Tim Duncan

Champion Basketball Star

Stew
Thornley

Enslow Publishers, Inc.
40 Industrial Road
Box 398
Berkeley Heights, NJ 07922
USA

http://www.enslow.com

Original edition published as *Super Sports Star Tim Duncan* in 2001.

Library of Congress Cataloging-in-Publication Data
Thornley, Stew.
 Tim Duncan : champion basketball star / Stew Thornley.
   p. cm. — (Sports star champions)
 Includes index.
 Summary: "Explores the life of San Antonio Spurs power forward Tim Duncan, including his childhood and college
career, his rise to stardom in the NBA, and his championship seasons with the Spurs"—Provided by publisher.
 ISBN 978-0-7660-4030-4
 1. Duncan, Tim, 1976—Juvenile literature. 2. Basketball players—United States—Biography—Juvenile literature.
I. Title.
 GV884.D86T57 2013
 796.323092—dc23
 [B]
                                                 2011050440
Future editions:
Paperback ISBN 978-1-4644-0160-2
ePUB ISBN 978-1-4645-1067-0
PDF ISBN 978-1-4646-1067-7

032012 Lake Book Manufacturing, Inc., Melrose Park, IL

Printed in the United States of America

10 9 8 7 6 5 4 3 2 1

To Our Readers: We have done our best to make sure all Internet addresses in this book were active and appropriate when we went to press. However, the author and the publisher have no control over and assume no liability for the material available on those Internet sites or on other Web sites they may link to. Any comments or suggestions can be sent by e-mail to comments@enslow.com or to the address on the back cover.

♻ Enslow Publishers, Inc., is committed to printing our books on recycled paper. The paper in every book contains 10% to 30% post-consumer waste (PCW). The cover board on the outside of each book contains 100% PCW. Our goal is to do our part to help young people and the environment too!

Illustration Credits: AP Images / Andres Leighton, pp. 12, 44; AP Images / Bob Jordan, p. 24; AP Images / Chuck Burton, p. 22; AP Images / David Zalubowski, p. 27; AP Images / Eric Gay, pp. 1, 4, 6, 9, 16, 38; AP Images / Jack Dempsey, p. 43; AP Images / Joe Cavaretta, p. 36; AP Images / Kathy Willens, p. 34; AP Images / LM Otero, p. 32; AP Images / Mark Lennihan, pp. 28, 30; AP Images / Matt Slocum, p. 8; AP Images / Tim Johnson, p. 5; AP Images / Timothy Easley, p. 20; AP Images / Tom Pidgeon, p. 18; AP Images / Tony Dejak, pp. 14, 40.

Cover Illustration: AP Images / Eric Gay (Tim Duncan).

Contents

Introduction

Tim Duncan has led the San Antonio Spurs to many NBA titles.

Tim Duncan is not afraid of much. He plays basketball against some of the biggest and toughest players in the National Basketball Association (NBA). He does not back down from those opponents. Duncan does have a few fears, though. He says he is scared of sharks. He is also afraid of looking down from high places.

Tim Duncan grew up on St. Croix, an island in the Caribbean Sea, about forty miles east of Puerto Rico. It is part of the Virgin Islands of the United States. Sharks are often in the waters around the island.

Duncan now plays for the San Antonio Spurs. He lives in Texas. Sharks are not a danger there. However, his other fear is one that he still must face. Looking down from high places is something he does every day. Duncan is seven feet tall. That is a long way from the ground.

Duncan deals with that fear. His height helps him to be one of the best players in the NBA. He loves to spend time on the practice court. He works hard to improve his skills and it pays off.

Tim Duncan's position on the basketball court is power forward. The job of a power forward is to score points. He also gets rebounds. It takes great strength to play this position. The area around the basket is full of defenders, usually large ones. It is not easy to score baskets in a crowd, and it takes a lot of muscle to grab rebounds. A power forward also has to be a good defensive player. Duncan can do all these things well. Duncan can also do a lot of other things that are not expected of a player his size. He is a good ball handler. He can also shoot from the outside. He loves to bank his shots off the backboard. He has a soft touch with his jump shots.

When Duncan joined the San Antonio Spurs in 1997, they already had a dominant big man, David Robinson. With both Duncan and Robinson on the floor at the same time, the Spurs were tough to beat. Duncan and Robinson won two NBA titles together. After Robinson retired, the Spurs continued to win titles with Duncan.

The Spurs won four NBA titles between 1999 and 2007. They had 42 different players on their championship teams. The only player on all four of those teams was Tim Duncan.

Tim Duncan is one of the best power forwards in NBA history.

Tim Duncan jumps to block a shot from LeBron James during the 2007 NBA Finals.

CHAPTER ONE

A Team Player

Tim Duncan was not having the best game of his life. The San Antonio Spurs were playing the Cleveland Cavaliers for the 2007 NBA championship. For the fourth time, Duncan was playing for a title.

In his first three NBA Finals, Duncan was named the Most Valuable Player (MVP). It wasn't likely he would get that honor again. Duncan was okay with that. He did not even mind that a player on the other team, LeBron James, was getting all the attention.

All that mattered to Duncan was that the Spurs win. He helped defend James in the first game of the series. In the second game, Duncan passed when he was being guarded by

Tim Duncan takes a shot during Game 2 of the NBA Finals on June 10, 2007. Duncan did not shoot his best during the series, but he still helped lead the Spurs to victory with his rebounding, defense, and passing.

two players at the same time. Being double-teamed meant someone else on the Spurs was open, and Duncan found him with a pass. San Antonio won both games.

The Spurs also won Game 3 and were only one win away from the championship.

Tim Duncan, holding the championship trophy, celebrates with teammate and Finals MVP Tony Parker (right) after winning the 2007 NBA title.

The fourth game was a close one. Guards Tony Parker and Manu Ginobili were the leading scorers for the Spurs. Duncan had a tougher night, making few of his shots.

However, Duncan is a leader regardless of how well he plays. His presence on the court inspires his teammates and gives them confidence. He also finds other ways to make an impact. Late in the game, he made a pass to center Fabricio Oberto, who scored to give the Spurs a six-point lead. Then he knocked the ball away from James, keeping the Cleveland star from a chance for a basket.

San Antonio won the game, 83–82, and claimed another championship.

Duncan praised his teammates, including Tony Parker, who was the Finals MVP. He also pointed out how well Spurs forward Bruce Bowen did guarding James. "Bruce did an awesome job of standing in front of that guy and making life tough for him," he said.

Most of all, Duncan talked of how the Spurs are a true team. "I didn't play the greatest," he said, "but we found a way to win. That's what this team is all about."

CHAPTER TWO

Life on an Island

Tim Duncan was a good athlete as he grew up.
But his first sport was not basketball. It was swimming. That
was what someone growing up in the Virgin Islands did.

Tim's parents helped their children with all the things
they did. His father, William, worked at different jobs. His
mother, Ione, was a midwife. She helped to deliver babies.
Ione also found time to go to her children's swimming races.
She even helped out with timing the races.

In 1989, Ione Duncan found out she had cancer. It was
very difficult, but she still worked at her job. She also kept
going to swimming races. "She was my biggest fan," said
Tim Duncan. "Every meet she was the loudest parent there.

Tim Duncan got his start playing basketball in the Virgin Islands after his father put up a hoop in the family's yard. In this photo, Duncan shoots over teammate Fabricio Oberto during a Spurs' training camp practice at the University of the Virgin Islands in October 2005.

Somehow I could always pick out her voice yelling over everyone else's."

The Duncans also had a basketball hoop on a pole in their yard. Tim's dad buried the pole very deep in the ground. Fierce storms with powerful, gusting winds sometimes hit the island. William Duncan did not want the pole and hoop to be blown over.

Tim still spent much more time swimming than shooting baskets. He dreamed of following his sister's path and swimming in the 1992 Olympics. That changed in September 1989 when Hurricane Hugo hit the island of St. Croix. The hurricane caused a lot of damage. It destroyed the large swimming pool where Tim and his team practiced. The team started practicing in the ocean. With his fear of sharks,

UP CLOSE!

Tim has two older sisters who were also great swimmers. One of them, Tricia, competed in the 1988 Olympics for the Virgin Islands. She swam in the 100-meter and 200-meter backstroke races.

Tim did not like that. He stopped going to swimming practice.

In April 1990, Ione Duncan died. Her death came one day before Tim's fourteenth birthday. Tim never swam in another race. "The hurricane broke Tim's routine by taking away our pool," said his older sister Tricia. "Then when Mom [died], he lost his motivation."

One thing that Hurricane Hugo did not destroy was the basketball hoop in the Duncans' yard. Tim's dad had done a good job putting it up. Tim began spending more time with the basketball.

Tim Duncan shoots during practice for the San Antonio Spurs. After Tim's mother died, he gave up swimming to focus on basketball. He began practicing with former college player Ricky Lowery.

He started playing basketball with Ricky Lowery, who was married to Tim's oldest sister, Cheryl. Lowery had played college basketball in Ohio. He taught Tim how to play. Lowery helped Tim learn how to shoot from the outside. That is a skill a smaller player needs. No one knew how tall Tim would become.

Tim grew quickly. By the time he was in his last year of high school, he was six feet eight inches tall. He was big enough to play close to the basket. Thanks to Lowery, Tim was also a good outside shooter. He became one of the top players on the team at St. Dunstan's Episcopal High School.

Tim started thinking about basketball as a way of getting an education. Before his mother died, she made each of her children promise to go to college. Tim was a good student, and he wanted to go to college. A scholarship, money awarded to students, was needed to help pay for college.

In the summer of 1992, Tim played against some top basketball players from the United States. A group of young players visited some of the islands in the Caribbean. One of the players was Alonzo Mourning. Mourning had been a great center at Georgetown University. He was the second player chosen in the 1992 NBA draft. The draft is the way NBA teams choose new players each year.

Tim Duncan, at six feet eight inches, towered over most players by his senior year of high school. He could dominate the game near the basket, but because of his practice with Ricky Lowery, he could also shoot from the outside. In this photo, Duncan takes a long jump shot during a playoff game against the Phoenix Suns.

Duncan played well against Mourning. The other players were impressed. One of those players was Chris King. He had played at Wake Forest University in North Carolina. When King got back home, he told Wake Forest's coach, Dave Odom, about Duncan.

Coach Odom visited St. Croix during Duncan's last season there. He thought Duncan was great. He asked Duncan to come to Wake Forest and play basketball. Duncan agreed.

Tim Duncan's dream of being an Olympic swimmer had ended. But he had another dream to follow. He would be going to college. He could continue his studies and also play basketball.

When Tim Duncan arrived at Wake Forest University, he made an immediate impact on the basketball team. Demon Deacons' fans knew they had a star in the making.

College Days

Tim Duncan studied psychology at Wake Forest. Psychology is the study of the human mind. It was a natural thing for Duncan to study. "I love to think," he said. "I just love the inner workings of the mind."

However, Wake Forest fans loved watching Tim Duncan play basketball.

Duncan received a lot of attention when he got to Wake Forest. Fans thought he would be a star on the court.

Tim Duncan's first game came in the Great Alaska Shootout. The Wake Forest Demon Deacons played against Alaska-Anchorage. Duncan did not score a single point. He did not even take a shot. But it did not take long for him to

Tim Duncan (left) smothers a shot during a game against the College of Charleston on March 17, 1994, in the NCAA Tournament. Duncan quickly became a menacing force on both offense and defense for the Demon Deacons. He was one of the nation's leading shot-blockers.

make an impact. He played in all of the Wake Forest games during his first year. His scoring average was 9.8 points per game. He also averaged 9.6 rebounds. Those are good totals for a first-year player.

But Tim Duncan was just getting warmed up. He started really playing well during his second season. His scoring average jumped by seven points. He also pulled down more rebounds. He ended up with the fifth-best rebounding average for college players in the country. He was very effective on defense, too. His long arms helped him swat away shots. He was one of the nation's top shot-blockers.

Wake Forest won its first two games in the NCAA Tournament in 1995. In the third game, Duncan did all he

UP CLOSE!

One of Tim Duncan's biggest fans is his sister Tricia. When her brother was in college, Tricia worked in Baltimore, Maryland. She drove down to North Carolina to watch her brother as often as she could. When Duncan was swimming, he could count on hearing his mother cheering for him. Now he could hear his sister do the same thing.

Although Tim Duncan could have been a top selection in the NBA draft, he elected to go back to school after the 1994–1995 college season. He wanted to finish school, and he continued to dominate on the court.

could to help his team win. He put on a great show at both ends of the court. He scored 12 points and pulled down 22 rebounds. He also blocked eight shots. But it was not enough. Wake Forest lost the game to Oklahoma State, 71–66.

Wake Forest University plays in the Atlantic Coast Conference (ACC). The ACC includes other teams like Duke, North Carolina, and Maryland. The conference had many talented players. A few of them entered the NBA draft after the 1994–1995 season. Rasheed Wallace and Jerry Stackhouse were chosen early in the draft. They were only second-year students, like Duncan. Unlike the others, Duncan did not take part in the draft that year, even though some people thought Duncan would have been the first player picked in the selection of pro players. But Duncan stayed at Wake Forest. He had to finish school.

Tim Duncan shoots over his defender during a game against Georgia Tech on February 25, 1997. Duncan was named to the All-American team in 1996 and earned an even more notable honor in 1997 when he was named college basketball's Player of the Year.

CHAPTER FOUR

Demon on the Court

Tim Duncan helped the Demon Deacons go even further in the 1996 NCAA playoffs. Wake Forest won its first two games. The Deacons then played Louisville. Louisville led by two points with a little more than a minute to play.

The Deacons knew they had to get the ball to Duncan. They could count on him. Duncan got the ball and spun toward the basket. A Louisville player slapped him on the arm as he took the shot. The ball still fell through the basket, and the game was tied. A foul was also called on the Louisville player who had slapped Duncan's arm. Duncan stepped up to the free-throw line, and he sank his shot.

That put the Deacons ahead, 60–59. There was no more scoring. Wake Forest won by one point. Duncan finished with 27 points.

Kentucky beat Wake Forest in the next game. It had been a great year for Duncan, though. He was named to the All-American team.

Duncan had one more year to play basketball in college. Although his team didn't win the national championship, he was named college basketball's Player of the Year in 1997. He was voted the country's best college defensive player, too. Duncan was also the best player in the history of Wake Forest. At the team's final home game, the school retired Duncan's number 21 jersey.

Tim Duncan was going into the NBA. And he had his college degree.

Duncan did not waste any time making a name for himself when he got to the NBA. Duncan got off to a great start with the San Antonio Spurs. He won the NBA's Rookie of the Year award. Just as in college, Duncan was getting awards. But he wanted much more. He wanted to play on a championship team.

Duncan had that chance the following year. The Spurs made it to the NBA Finals and played the New York Knicks.

After the San Antonio Spurs selected Tim Duncan number one overall in the NBA draft, he became an immediate superstar. In this photo, Duncan stands with teammate David Robinson during his first NBA game against the Denver Nuggets on October 31, 1997.

Tim Duncan soars high above a crowd of defenders to take a shot during Game 4 of the 1999 NBA Finals at Madison Square Garden. Duncan controlled the paint during the series, and the Knicks had a very difficult time preventing the Spurs' star from scoring.

The first two games were played in San Antonio. Duncan and the Spurs won the first game. Duncan had 33 points and 16 rebounds.

Duncan played well in the second game, which the Spurs also won. Then the teams went to New York. On their home court, the Knicks won Game 3. Duncan said the loss helped the Spurs to focus.

The fourth game was close. The Spurs opened up a lead in the second half. But the Knicks did not quit. New York got to within two points of San Antonio. There were just over three minutes left in the game. Now it was time for defense.

Larry Johnson of the Knicks went up for a shot. He did not have a chance. Both Duncan and David Robinson blocked his shot. The Spurs won by seven points.

In the fifth game, Duncan displayed all his great moves. He made jump-hook shots and turnaround fadeaway jump shots. Almost every shot he took seemed to drop through the basket.

However, the Knicks stayed close and had a one-point lead with less than a minute left to play. Avery Johnson of the Spurs lobbed a pass inside. Duncan grabbed the pass. He was guarded closely by Larry Johnson of the Knicks.

Tim Duncan raises the NBA Finals MVP trophy as he celebrates with his teammates after defeating the New York Knicks for the NBA championship.

Duncan passed the ball back out to teammate Sean Elliott. Elliott passed to Avery Johnson in the left corner. Johnson fired a jump shot that was nothing but net. It gave the Spurs a 78–77 lead.

The Spurs held the one-point lead into the final seconds of the game. The Knicks had the ball out of bounds with 2.1 seconds left. Charlie Ward threw an inbound pass to Latrell Sprewell under the basket. However, Elliott and Duncan trapped Sprewell. He had to dribble away. He tried a jump shot from near the baseline at the end of the court. Duncan and Robinson swarmed toward Sprewell as he took the shot. The shot fell short. The buzzer sounded to end the game, and the Spurs were NBA champions.

Tim Duncan finished the game with 31 points and 9 rebounds. He averaged 27.4 points and 14 rebounds per game in the series against the Knicks. For that, he was voted the Most Valuable Player of the NBA Finals.

Duncan liked that, but he was even more excited about his team winning the NBA championship!

Tim Duncan goes up for a basket against Boston Celtics superstar Kevin Garnett during the NBA All-Star Game on February 14, 2010. Duncan has been chosen for the All-Star team in almost every season of his career.

More Titles

Duncan was off to a great start in his career. In addition to getting a championship ring, he was named to the NBA's first-team All-Defensive team.

He had a knee injury near the end of the 1999–2000 season and had to have surgery. Duncan came back strong in the following seasons. He and David Robinson continued to team up as a tough combination to beat.

In 2002, Duncan had an amazing performance in the All-Star Game. He started the game and had 14 points and 14 rebounds. His entire season was great. Duncan was among the top five players in scoring, rebounding, and blocked shots. He was an awesome player on offense and defense.

Tim Duncan blocks a shot against New Jersey Nets center Dikembe Mutombo during a NBA Finals game on June 11, 2003. Not only did Duncan lead the Spurs to the 2003 NBA title, he also collected his second-consecutive MVP trophy.

Duncan won the NBA's Most Valuable Player award that season. He was named to the first-team All-Defensive team for the fourth year in a row.

The 2002–2003 season would be the last for David Robinson. He was going to retire at the end of the year. Duncan and the Spurs wanted to help him win another title before he left.

Duncan had another huge year and was named the MVP for the second year in a row. The last player to win back-to-back MVP awards was Chicago Bulls guard Michael Jordan.

UP CLOSE!

In addition to playing in the NBA, Duncan had the opportunity to play for the United States. It was during the Olympic Games in 2004 in Athens, Greece. He was teammates with LeBron James, Allen Iverson, Carmelo Anthony, and Dwyane Wade. Normally, he played against these superstars. Duncan shot well in the Olympics and rebounded even better. He tied a record for the most total rebounds in the Olympics.

Tim Duncan snatches a rebound and looks for an open teammate during Game 2 of the 2005 NBA Finals. The San Antonio Spurs defeated the Detroit Pistons in a competitive seven-game series to give Duncan his third NBA title.

The Spurs made it back to the NBA Finals and beat the New Jersey Nets, four games to two. Again, Duncan was named the Finals MVP.

"Winning the NBA championship was special in so many ways," Duncan said. "One of the biggest thrills was playing the final minutes with David Robinson. To be able to send him off that way was huge for us and for him."

Robinson was gone, but the Spurs still had Duncan and other good players. Some people questioned whether the team could win a championship without David Robinson. They wondered if Duncan was good enough on his own.

In 2005, that question was answered. The Spurs played the Detroit Pistons for the championship. Duncan was the only player still on the Spurs from the 1999 title team. The series went the limit. In the seventh game, Detroit led in the third quarter. Duncan helped the Spurs come back. He scored 12 points in the quarter. As the Pistons double-teamed him, Duncan passed to open teammates.

San Antonio won, 81–74. Duncan was the Finals MVP for the third time. He showed he could win without Robinson. And the one person who knew that he could was David Robinson, who said, "Tim Duncan doesn't need to prove anything to me."

Tim Duncan glides toward the basket for a slam dunk during a game on January 21, 2011. Although Duncan played with many different teammates, his consistent greatness helped the Spurs win four championships in nine seasons.

Duncan and the Spurs still weren't done. In 2007, they beat the Cleveland Cavaliers to win another title. From 1999 to 2007, the Spurs won four championships. During that time, forty-two players were on the Spurs. The one constant was Tim Duncan.

The coach for the Spurs during that time was Gregg Popovich. "Each championship has a personality of its own," he said, "but obviously watching Tim Duncan be a common thread through it all is especially satisfying. Sometimes he's the best player, sometimes he's not, but he's the common denominator for the whole group."

Tim Duncan has led the San Antonio Spurs to twelve straight years of at least fifty regular-season wins.

Under the Radar

The Spurs haven't won any more titles since 2007, but they have continued to be a great team. In 2010–2011, San Antonio had the best regular-season record in the NBA and won at least fifty games for the twelfth straight year.

What stood out about the Spurs is how well they play together. Even though Duncan is their superstar, the other players are just as important. Duncan knows that. His teammate Tony Parker said, "He can score, rebound, block shots, and everything, but he's unselfish enough to trust his teammates. He knows he can't win by himself."

Duncan is one of the best players ever. Jeff Van Gundy, who has coached in the NBA, said, "In my 20 years in the

Tim Duncan high fives a student during a visit to the after-school program Family Life at the University of the Virgin Islands in St. Thomas. Duncan is a leader off the court, too, supporting many important causes. His foundation focuses on health awareness, education, and recreation in San Antonio, Winston-Salem (North Carolina), and the U.S. Virgin Islands.

Duncan doesn't seek recognition for himself or his team. "We're under the radar every year," Duncan said of the Spurs. "That's where we like to be. At the end of the day it's all about winning games and championships, and we've done that."

Career Statistics

NBA Regular-Season Statistics With San Antonio Spurs

Year	GP	Min.	FGM	FGA	FG%	FT%	Reb.	Ast.	Stl.	Blk.	Pts.	PPG
1997–1998	82	3,204	706	1,287	.549	.662	977	224	55	206	1,731	21.1
1998–1999	50	1,963	418	845	.495	.690	571	121	45	126	1,084	21.7
1999–2000	74	2,875	628	1,281	.490	.761	918	234	66	165	1,716	23.2
2000–2001	82	3,174	702	1,406	.499	.618	997	245	70	192	1,820	22.2
2001–2002	82	3,329	764	1,504	.508	.799	1042	307	61	203	2,089	25.5
2002–2003	81	3,181	714	1,392	.513	.710	1043	316	55	237	1,884	23.3
2003–2004	68	2,527	592	1,181	.501	.599	859	213	62	185	1,538	22.3
2004–2005	66	2,203	517	1,042	.496	.670	732	179	45	174	1,342	20.3
2005–2006	80	2,784	574	1,185	.484	.629	881	253	70	162	1,485	18.6
2006–2007	80	2,725	618	1,131	.546	.637	846	273	66	190	1,599	20.0
2007–2008	78	2,651	585	1,178	.497	.730	881	218	56	152	1,508	19.3
2008–2009	75	2,523	558	1,107	.504	.692	800	264	38	126	1,450	19.3
2009–2010	78	2,438	561	1,082	.518	.725	788	246	45	117	1,395	17.9
2010–2011	76	2,156	419	838	.500	.716	678	203	50	146	1,022	13.4
Totals	1,053	37,733	8,356	16,459	.508	.688	12,013	3,296	784	2,381	21,663	20.6

GP–Games Played
Min.–Minutes Played
FGM–Field Goals Made

FGA–Field Goals Attempted
FG%–Field Goal Percentage
FT%–Free Throw Percentage

Reb.–Rebounds
Ast.–Assists
Stl.–Steals

Blk.–Blocked Shots
Pts.–Points Scored
PPG–Points per Game

Where to Write to Tim Duncan

Mr. Tim Duncan
c/o San Antonio Spurs
One AT&T Center
San Antonio, TX 78219

Glossary

bank shot—A shot that bounces (or banks) off the backboard.

baseline—The out-of-bounds line that runs behind the basket.

double-teaming—Two defenders guarding one player.

draft—The way NBA teams choose new players each year.

dunk—A shot that is slammed through the basket from directly above the basket. Also known as a slam or slam dunk.

fadeaway jumper—A shot taken while falling away from the basket.

jump hook—A one-handed shot taken while jumping.

NCAA Tournament—The national college tournament. NCAA stands for National Collegiate Athletic Association.

outside shot—A shot taken a long distance away from the basket.

rebound—Grabbing the basketball after a missed shot.

triple double—Getting double figures (ten or more) in three different offensive and/or defensive categories in a game.

turnaround—A shot taken after the player shooting the ball has turned to face the basket.

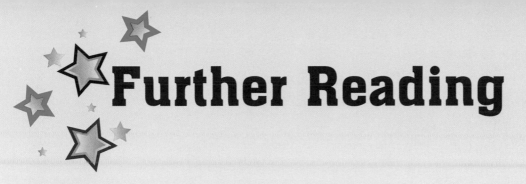

Further Reading

Books

Bednar, Chuck. *Tim Duncan.* Philadelphia: Mason Crest Publishers, 2009.

Doeden, Matt. *The World's Greatest Basketball Players.* Mankato, Minn.: Capstone Press, 2010.

Roselius, J. Chris. *San Antonio Spurs.* Minneapolis, Minn.: ABDO Publishing Co., 2011

Savage, Jeff. *Tim Duncan.* Minneapolis, Minn.: Lerner Publications Co., 2010.

Walters, John. *Tim Duncan.* Chanhassen, Minn.: Child's World, 2007.

Internet Addresses

ESPN.com: Tim Duncan Player Profile
<http://espn.go.com/nba/player/_/id/215/tim-duncan>

The Official Web site of the San Antonio Spurs
<http://www.nba.com/spurs/>

Slamduncan.com: The Official Web site of Tim Duncan
<http://www.slamduncan.com/>

Index